TO FATYONEN

To Fatyonen

Our Teenage Sister and Friend

Dominic Asedeh
Achsah Asedeh

AFRICA CHRISTIAN TEXTBOOKS

2017

Africa Christian Textbooks (ACTS)

ACTS Bookshop, International HQ, TCNN,
PMB 2020, Bukuru, Plateau State, 930008, Nigeria
GSM: +234 (0) 803-589-5328; E-mail: pa@actsnigeria.org
Website: http://actsnigeria.org

ISBN: 9789789053773 Print
ISBN: 9789789053780 ePub
ISBN: 9789789053797 Mobi

CONTENTS

FORWARD

As teens grow, hormones rage and bodies change dramatically. Most teens are left in a state of confusion with voices of authority strangely silent on the topic. They turn to their friends who are often misinformed or who approach the topic with giggles or lewdness, leaving teens wondering what to do with their budding sexuality. Sadly, our teenagers experiment with sex and have little understanding of why they feel the strange ways they do or act in ways they can't explain or even control.

Dominic and Achsah combined their efforts to provide teenage girls with answers for the journey through the turbulent waters of adolescence. They offer straightforward answers to what is happening biologically within a girl's body at puberty, explain how girls can take care of themselves appropriately, warn against unwise sexual involvement, and encourage them to relate to boys wisely.

One of my favourite parts of this tasteful book is how they discussed the emotional turbulence all teens face as they negotiate adolescence and all the changes that are going on which cause so much confusion and problems. The authors offer practical and realistic advice to both boys and girls to overcome anxiety, anger, depression, and fears that they face during their teen years. Another chapter deals with building a healthy self-esteem, especially for women who compete at a disadvantage in our male-dominated Nigerian culture.

Who of us wouldn't have benefitted from such helpful advice as a teenager on how to choose good friends and establish meaningful relationships as a young person? Using biblical principles, Dominic and Achsah address this topic using interesting examples from the lives of other people who have been influenced by positive and negative friendships.

The authors offer helpful advice on how to explore certain career options and work toward reasonable goals which will help any older teen deal with these life-altering decisions. They also encourage young people to make the most important decision of their lives: choosing which master they will serve through life. They explain the way to salvation clearly and candidly; furthermore, they concisely offer help to teens to keep their relationship with God sweet and growing.

I first met Dominic as his English teacher at Jos ECWA Theological Seminary, Jos, Nigeria. He was a diligent student who showed a flair for writing and the pursuit of excellence in his studies. It was a joy to see his Christian character also grow with his academic pursuits. It was my joy and privilege to help him through the editing process of his writing adventure. He patiently worked hard to make this helpful book a reality--and one that was worth publishing and placing into the hands of every teenage girl.

As a guest in Nigeria and a keen observer of culture, one disturbing observation I have made is how little emphasis is given to helping teenagers understand their bodies and how to handle their sexuality. We leave teens to figure everything out on their own. When I have asked Nigerian women where they received their sex information, most told me they received little or no explanation from their parents, even on menstruation, or they received faulty or inaccurate information from their friends who didn't know much more than themselves! Some reported feeling fearful and confused when they started bleeding for no reason; too often no one had told them of the completely normal process of growing up and the path to the maturation of the reproductive system.

Most parents either still consider sex a taboo subject and refuse to talk openly about it, or they are too embarrassed to address the surrounding issues with their children at any age. Our teens often are told in our churches and youth fellowships "Don't have sex!" with little explanation of the precious gift God has given them. The silence of godly adults on this subject is leaving teens to figure out on their own what is appropriate or inappropriate behaviour. Ungodly influences fill in the gaps and pressure our kids to experiment with sex, to give in to what their bodies are calling them to do, or to lie to them that "Everyone is doing it" or the age old "If you loved me, you would let me show my love to you."

We must rise to the challenge, provide wholesome, accurate information, and HELP our teens to embrace a healthy, biblical attitude to their sexuality. We need to be understanding of the changes raging within them and guide them supportively through the turbulence of adolescence with sensitivity.

This book is a start to offer teen girls answers not only to the way their bodies function but how to deal with all the emotions that come along with hormonal changes of puberty. It is written in a friendly style with a wholesome and honest approach to discuss openly what all teens need to be aware of. I would use it to guide her thinking BEFORE puberty arrives, opening the door of discussion between mother and daughter on this sensitive but important topic where parents need to take the lead in educating their own children about human development.

Thank you Dominic and Achsah for writing this wonderful tool to help our teenage girls become all they can be and for presenting the topics in an understandable, inviting manner. I pray it will be well received and widely used to make a stronger Nigeria that we all can enjoy.

Heidi Jessurun, R.N., B.A.
SIM, Nigeria
Lecturer at JETS in Christian Home,
Children & Youth, English, Study Habits

PREFACE

We chose the name of the book *To Fatyonen, Our Teenage Sister and Friend* for a number of reasons. First, Fatyonen is a (prayer) native name literally meaning "God, let her live." Having lost two female children at tender ages, her parents prayed to God for her to live, and he answered. The authors join in to play their part in her life, praying that she will not just live, but that her living becomes a blessing not just to her family alone, but to her generation at large. Hence, the prayer for the book is that as this young lady grows into becoming a blessing, her life will be a positive example to others through the advice, encouragement and challenges given in this book.

Furthermore, the later part of the name resulted because she (Fatyonen) is both a biological sister and a friend to both authors.

The teenage years are among the most challenging years in life, as one grows into adulthood. In addition to that, it is the time of life where teens need a lot of good advice and counseling because, mistakes made at this stage might live on to haunt one in the future. It is in this light that we pray that Fatyonen and as many as shall read this book long after she is grown past the teenage years, will heed the counsel therein. This piece is hence released to shape the future of our great country Nigeria, Africa and the whole world at large.

God's blessing,
Dominic and Achsah Asedeh
October 2017

APPRECIATION

Our foremost and deepest appreciation goes to God for initiating, guiding and sustaining this work to the end.

Our heartfelt gratitude goes to the following people: Mr. & Mrs. Danjuma Asedeh, Mr. & Mrs. Ahmadu Madaki, Grace Bebeyi, Nuhu B. Gaina, Nehemiah Giwa, Samson Bulus *Aka* C-free, Sulmane Barje Maigadi, Rev. James B. Francis, Dr. Cephas T.A. Tushima, Dr. Mrs. Rose Galadima, Prof. George Janvier, Rev. Benjamin Gaina, Mrs. Erasmus Sule of FCS Gombe State and Mrs. Dituweh Yohanah Mamman who has been part of this project from its early days. Thank you for your prayers, support, encouragement, challenges and other numerous invaluable contributions towards the success of this project.

Big thanks also to Mrs. Elizabeth Mislum Ishaya who composed the poem "Natural Flowers."

Thank you Mrs. Heidi Jessurun for taking on the task to proofread the manuscript of this book, and for making the needed guidance to give this book purpose and direction; thank you for your patience and sacrifice.

God bless you all.

A WORD TO PARENTS

As you will discover in this piece, we have encouraged teenagers to be **open**. This is because it is in being open that they can receive the help. However, some part of our African culture (shame to be precise) make these teens unwilling to be open to us. Sometimes we criticize them and make them feel worse, as a result some of them would prefer to talk with their fellow peers or others than to their parents. Hence our humble appeal is for a change in mindset, do not make them feel bad about themselves when they ask you questions or open up about how they feel. Rather, patiently take the time to guide them and give them all the necessary support they need.

Teenage is a phase of God's wonder in human development as the body and mind transition to adulthood. With all its beauty and awe, it can also be a period of frustration for both the teenagers and those around them, especially their parents. The reality is that hormonal transitional configurations are making teenagers feel and act differently, while parents may still be seeing and treating the teenager as their home baby. Almost with certainty, the teenage may respond with rebellion and at same time try to send the message which communicates almost non verbally that: "I am not a child anymore, don't you know or can't you see?"

To help the teenage girl or boy, fighting back to assert parental control isn't the solution. What your teenage boy or girl needs at this point is guidance, not supervision. They need you to understand the changes and help them learn how best to cope with these realities in their human biological development. This collective guidance and responsibility falls on the parents and the community. In Africa a proverb says: "It takes a village to raise a child."

In many communities of Africa, it is either taboo or considered very embarrassing to talk about sex. Children grow into their teenage years as one slips into a river unexpectedly without prior preparation on how to swim their way back to safety ashore. As they swim, frantically, if the parents or guardians do not play an active role of walking with them through teenage turbulences, they just may take any help that comes; anything that might offer them a life line; whatever will help them understand where they are in that state of mind and body. That "help" could come from their equally clueless friends, media or ill-intentioned adults who may end up taking advantage of them.

The Revd Gideon Para-Mallam
IFES, Regional Secretary

NATURAL FLOWER

Poetry has always likened the female to
a flower;
She is beautiful and colorful. She has a sweet smell of
enchantment.
Think of spring, summer and winter flowers,
Think of houseplants, garden plants, desert flowers,
Tropical flowers,
Flowers that grow in sun or shade.
Flowers that grow in clusters or single blossoms,
Flowers with fine stems or strong stalks,
Think of large flowers, tiny flowers of trees.
It doesn't matter the climate or weather,
Every female remains the symbol of beauty.
For the flower you are,
I love to watch you grow,
Your maturity so fascinating, your beauty so tender,
Yet fragile.
My concern, so strong, I fret,
I cherish your innocence and fear your ignorance.
Soon you will have lots of choices to make,
Friendships, silver and gold,
Many will offer for your future in return.
But I am hopeful that you will be prayerful, and careful,
Trade not your beauty 'cos' you are precious.
You've come a long way,
I must say, I am proud of you.
You are so cool.

—Mrs. Elizabeth Mislum Ishaya

HELLO

It is with much joy and gladness of heart that we write this letter to you. We had longed to write before now, but too many things got in the way. However, now that we have the opportunity, we feel privileged and honoured to do so. Actually, if we'd written this letter to you earlier than now, it might not have made a lot of sense to you. This is because there is a time for everything, and now is the best time to let you in on the things you need to know about growing up.

Growth and development are necessary for life. A Fulani man wants his cattle to increase in number, a farmer wants to have a larger harvest than he had before. A business woman wants her business to grow further, and a student wants to be promoted in class. Even civil servants and other workers want to be promoted in their work places too. You see, people want to be better than they were before.

However, growth and development don't just occur without thought and, at times, challenge. You are growing up, and you may face challenges regarding issues like friends, sex, career, self-esteem and lots more. Therefore, we are writing this letter to encourage, help and guide you in your growing process. We also want to provide you with tips you might need to know about these things. We hope to help you reflect on who you were before now, to help you see clearer who you are now and to make you aware and prepare you for the future.

As you read, you will come across places where it is written "I." This is because one of us has individually written that section. In the places where "we" is used, it simply means we both have written the section together.

We pray that God will give you understanding about the things we will be communicating to you. We also pray that he will give you the wisdom to make the best use of this information in becoming the **BEST** teenager you can be. Amen.

CHAPTER 1

GROWING UP

I want to be a teacher someday, so I'm seizing this opportunity to try out my talent; you're my new student. There are things I want to educate you about. Some might not be new while others might be entirely strange. I hope you will enjoy my experimental lectures. You see, I have noticed a process in women that I will call "The General Change Phenomenon." Lectures begin:

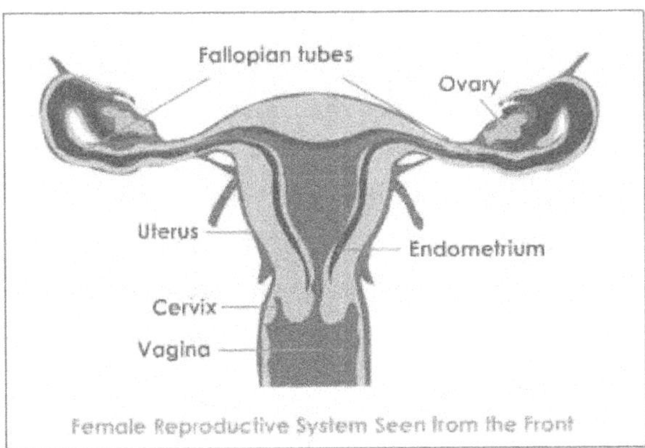

Photo credit: Tutorvista.com

The above picture is the representation of the system in women whether young or old, designed to help them produce babies. There are many organs that are not visible in the picture, but as I explain, I will try to make you understand those unseen parts and their functions as well. Scientists tell us that every unborn female baby has plenty, albeit very tiny, eggs inside her abdomen. As the unborn baby develops in her mother's womb, the **EGGS** inside her will change. When the baby girl is eventually born she will be born with about 2,000,000 (2 million) of these tiny eggs inside a part of her reproductive system called the **OVARIES**.

Scientists also agree that as this infant girl grows up, some of these 2,000,000 eggs will die. However, their dying will not affect the girl. By the time the girl has grown to be about 12-14 years, almost 1,960,000 eggs would have died, leaving only about 40,000 in her ovaries.

As soon as she gets to this stage, a **gland** in her brain will produce and release some special chemicals called **HORMONES**. Scientists say that this happens to prepare the girl's body for changes and development. Some of these changes and developments may include the swelling of her breasts, growth of hair in her armpit and pubic regions, change in voice sound, increase in height, increase in hips and buttocks size, etc. All these are what medical personnel call signs of **PUBERTY** or **ADOLESCENCE**.

At this age, something interesting starts to happen. You know when fruits get ripened they begin to fall from the tree on their own. Similarly, the ripe eggs in the ovaries will be released one after another over a period of time. The periodic release of these eggs is called **OVULATION**.

At the release of each ripe egg, some special chemicals called **PROGESTERONE** are produced and released from the brain. The hormone released into the girl's body will prepare the womb or **UTERUS** for welcoming the released ripe egg; the womb's wall is lined with a thick material called **ENDOMETRIUM**. The expected guest will keep coming gradually through the **FALLOPIAN TUBE**. The ripe egg becomes like a **VIP** (Very Important Person).

Now, assuming the governor says he will be coming to your school, and in the process, commission a new set of classes. You would be very excited, wouldn't you? I am sure even your teachers would be very excited. They would ask you to sweep the entire school compound, decorate the school with ribbons, flowers and balloons. You would be directed to wipe glasses and clean furniture. You might even display a big banner which may read something like, "You are welcome to our school, Your Excellency." I can bet that all of you would be neatly dressed in your washed and ironed uniforms, fitted with white socks and sandals. And, everyone will wait patiently until the guest has arrived.

Let's assume he did come to the school, greeted you all, but did not commission anything due to some other reasons, but promised to come back again next year. What do you think will happen to all the flowers, decorations, ribbons, banners and the rest? They will all be removed, won't they? Of course, you will remove them all and begin to look forward to the governor's second coming.

Scientists say that, in a similar way, when the ripe egg released from the ovaries comes through the fallopian tube into the uterus or womb and does not get fertilized, it will leave. All the decorations [thick linings] in the womb will be removed and flushed out in the form of blood. The flushing out of blood through the girl's vagina is called **MENSTRUATION** or **MENSES**. This flow of blood may last for 4-7 days, at intervals within the days. So, the time the ripe egg is released (i.e. ovulation) up to the time when the blood is flushed out (i.e. menstruation) is what is scientifically known as the **MENSTRUAL CYCLE**. The entire cycle usually lasts for about 26-32 days.

This process is the gift of God and is how He designed women. It is not dirty but it should be accompanied by good hygienic habits. During the period of the menses, you may experience backache, feelings of nausea, lower abdominal pains, and cramps. There could also be feelings of being tired and stressed out and, at times, you may get pimples. You may also become moody or irritable. During this period, you are to take your bath regularly, use sanitary pads (not tissue papers), and don't use perfumes or powder on your private parts. Some women say that drinking hot water or tea, using pain reliever like Panadol when necessary will be of help.

So how do women become pregnant? To understand this we turn to **FERTILIZATION**. When a man and a woman have sexual intercourse, the man enters his hardened, erect penis inside the woman's vagina. After movement that brings pleasure, the man will release whitish liquid called **SEMEN**, which contains **SPERM CELLS**. These sperm cells or semen released from the man's penis into the woman's vagina might number up to about 1,000,000 (1 million) or more. If at the time of their release, there happens to be a ripe egg that has been released from the ovary of the woman, the sperm cells will swim up to the ripe egg in the womb and encircle it.

Each one of the sperm cells will struggle to enter into the matured egg, and the sperm cell that is strong enough to enter the egg first, is said to have fertilized the egg. All the other sperm cells will die and then fertilization will have taken place; the woman will be pregnant. In case two sperm cells enter into the ripe egg at the same time, the woman may give birth to twins. If three enter, there will be triplets. However, if one sperm divides itself into two in the process of fertilization, the woman will give birth to a set of identical twins, and both will be of the same sex; either boys or girls.

Another interesting thing is that when a woman gets to the age of 45-50 years, she will cease releasing ripening eggs because her hormones change. As a result, she will neither menstruate nor be able to get pregnant again. This period is called **MENOPAUSE**.

You too will come to experience most of these changes. If I'm not mistaken, you have begun experiencing some of it. As you continue to grow, you will come to discover more for yourself. Physically, emotionally, mentally, psychologically and in other areas you will experience further changes. You will become a woman.

Therefore, like I'd earlier written, no growth and development as such happens without challenges. You will experience these good, God-given phenomena but at the same time, there will be danger lurking around. Some girls have been uninformed, or simply careless, and have become victims of circumstances. I am writing you now so that you can know the challenges that come during the teen age years and to prepare you against the pitfalls along the way.

You see, as you keep on developing and maturing, there will be a lot of changes within you. You will begin to be mindful of dressing more neatly; by concentrating more on your hair, and you might need more cosmetics, perfumes and creams. It is also possible that you will begin to spend more time with your friends discussing girls' stuff like films, music, fashion, and boys and so on. Your attention might turn to yourself and the things you like and make you happy. You will also desire to become in charge of your choices and your decisions. In this regards however, remember that not all choices and decisions you make will be the best for you; hence Dad, mum, uncles, aunts and teachers are available to help guide and shape you.

Resisting Temptation

Furthermore, temptations of different types will come to you; some may be obvious, while others will be indirect, cunning and deceitful. Look, you might be tempted to give flimsy excuses to escape household chores. You might also begin to feel Mum or your teachers are overworking you and do not want to give you time out with your friends. As a result, you will eagerly desire for a time-out in the space where you are away from all of it, except for you and your friends, having all the fun you can. You may feel eager to indulge in snacks and junk food. You may also be tempted to desire everything your friends have and imitate them in everything. You may begin to find it hard to keep lock and key over your feelings, desires and emotions. You may also have the feeling of being right in everything; always insisting on having things done your own way. Are you getting it?

Temptations will assume different forms and patterns. You have to know and address them as temptations. At times, you may want to disrespect those more elderly than yourself. It may come to the point where you may find it hard to listen to advice, correction, instruction, rebuke and discipline, simply because they don't fit into your new ways. Why do you think girls steal from others and some run away from home, and some fight, at times, with their parents? It is because they have followed these temptations without being careful. Others find it hard to choose between their parents' and their friends' advice. All these and lots more will come your way but when they finally do, (as they already have in some ways) don't be afraid or panic.

Openness

Whatever it is that comes your way now, do not be in a hurry to conclude that it is good or bad. There are some that you might not understand but since you are already gaining control over your decision making senses, what is likely to happen is this. You may begin to trust yourself and may want to keep things to yourself. You may feel like you can take care of such things on your own even without the help of others. That won't help you. In fact, the secret to overcoming and doing the right thing at such times is ***openness***.

Openness is being willing to talk to others about your personal matters the way they are; being frank and sincere. I am not advising you to make a public show of your matters. No! Rather, what I am calling you to do is this: when faced with confusing choices and decisions or even when you are very sure, go to elderly ones whom you trust and who trust you too, those whom you know are good and respectable. Talk with them (these include: Dad, Mum, good and close aunts). Let them advise you about what to do. Do not be in a hurry to tell friends about your problems because friends may only misguide you (Proverbs 13:20).

Seeking for counsel sincerely from those ahead of you requires humility and wisdom. If you learn from the wise, you are certain to become wise, and you will successfully grow through this sweet but challenging stage in life.

Discussion Points

1. List some of the things discussed in this chapter which you have known before.
2. List and discuss some new things you have learnt from reading this chapter.
3. Discuss other possible changes in teen girls you know
4. Discuss in your group/club some of the challenges and temptations you currently experience right now.
5. Have you been open to older ones about things you are going through? If no, why not? If yes, how helpful is it?
6. Consider your relationship with your parents. If you feel uncomfortable talking to them openly, it may be helpful to write a letter to your parents to help you "rehearse" what you would like to ask them about, or describe how you would like them to respond to your questions. You don't need to give them the letter, but it can be helpful to write out your feelings about your relationship with them or describe how you would like to be more open with them. It can also help you think more clearly about the questions you have about all the changes occurring in your body during adolescence. What would your letter include?

CHAPTER 2

SEX AND YOU

Angel had a boyfriend, Freddy. Her mother, who was a widow, cautioned her about the way she goes about with him. Her mother would often say to her,

> Angel, you can be friends with Freddy, but please when you notice that he or any other person begins to do or suggest things that will lead you to sex, please try to avoid such.

As time went on Angel turned out to be pregnant. Her mother sat her down and asked her who she had sex with, and Angel said it was Freddy. Once at Freddy's house when there was no one home, he began to touch her body and do things to her which were exciting; and eventually led to sex. Angel explained that she could not tell her mother because she was afraid of what her mother would say and do. And they both agreed not to do it again. However, as they continued to find themselves where there was no one they always did something which eventually will lead to sex.

Freddy, who was himself a teenager, could not cater for the financial and other needs of Angel in her pregnant state. So, Angel's mother, with the support of Freddy's parents, gave her all the support she needed to deliver safely. Her mother and other relations tried to make her understand that she can still live up to her potential despite the situation she found herself in, that is if she will be determined to put aside further involvement in premarital sex and focus on her education. Freddy was terrified at being a teenage father and was unwilling to continue to be friends with Angel.

After Angel delivered her child, she put her mind back to study and to live right. She later graduated from University and got married. She lives as a happily married woman with three children, supporting her family and using her time and resources to help other teenagers who may be in danger of making the mistakes she made.

Self-Control

The challenges are too many to be counted. My prayer is that you will stand through them all. Although it is natural that they come, you must know that because they are natural does not mean it is also natural to respond and agree with their impulse. If you take good care of yourself, you will become more attractive especially to the opposite sex, **the boys**. They will come. Your age mates, classmates and even those older than you, will come to you to ask for your name, to sit close to you, seek to talk or argue with you, to keep you company, etc. You will make friends; boys and girls, at school, in church and around the neighborhood. Some of them will visit you at home. If you ask me, this is supposed to happen.

However, this is where the danger lies. You are on the highway to destruction when you begin to give in to wrong advice, listening to friends' voices rather than the advice of your parents and guardians, and when you begin to dress immodestly. Equally destructive is exposing your body to people, or if you begin to allow boys to touch you, hold you and turn you into their toy, and if you begin to allow your emotions to control you instead of you being in control.

What I have discovered is that girls who fall into such temptations during their teens do not usually find it easy to cope with life again. Although a few may find the courage and strength to repent and continue the good life (like the case of Angel), they don't usually find it easy to do so. Most end up being dragged into deeper troubled waters. Others become carriers of sexually transmitted diseases such as HIV/AIDS, syphilis, genital warts, and viruses that may later cause cervical cancer. Those who drop out of school without qualifications, and/or who run away from home, often end up abusing drugs and engaging in crime and prostitution just to have enough money to live on. Others may appear to be doing well, but privately indulge in sexual perversions, which in turn can create havoc with personal relationships. Dreams of a happy, stable family life remain just that – dreams. A lot end their lives miserably. I'm sure you don't want to live or end up like any of these. So please, pay attention to my warnings.

Sexual Desires

I believe deep down in me that it will be appropriate if I should write to you more extensively on the issue of sex. Do you wonder why people talk so much about sex? This is because it has become more of a religion today, gaining the support and approval of people all over the world. The media is now highly promoting it just to entice people. It is so tempting and appealing that people are easily deceived into it without consideration.

Listen, when one is a teenager, or even an adult, there will always be a sexual urge or desire that arises. This is the way God designed it to be to ensure that we reproduce. However, sex is also a gift designed to be enjoyed within the bounds of marriage only. Teens (even adults) have difficulty controlling their desires. The reason is this: the teen years (pre-adolescence) is when the male and female sex cells become developed and begin to mature. So there is usually a strong desire to want to experiment. At some point, you too will feel the desire for sex. It is normal to feel that way, but you must control it and not let it control you. Marriage is the only proper place to express our God-given sexual desires.

The temptation can be so strong that teenagers lose their sense of control. They search until they have found someone with whom to have sex. That is why the issue of "boyfriend" and "girlfriend" is so rampant at this period. My dear, be wise. The mistake usually begins with holding hands, shoulders or hips, then hugging, staying in dark corners, then kissing, touching body parts and, before you know it, you've sold yourself out at a cheap price that will fetch you no value but invites regret and guilt. To make matters worse, often, although not always, the boy or man who succeeds in messing up a girl, goes about telling his friends that he has "finished with 'that girl,'" thus destroying any good reputation she had and making it appear she is immoral and promiscuous. I pray "that girl" will not be you.

You see dear, engaging in any activity that leads to sex before or outside of marriage is not part of God's beautiful design for human sexuality. The Bible makes it clear that sexual immortality is morally wrong and we know it has serious consequences on our bodies and in society. Let me explain more fully some of the consequences of irresponsible sexual behaviour:

- You will risk being infected with fatal diseases such as HIV/AIDS and other harmful sexually transmitted diseases.
- There is the risk of becoming pregnant and parenting at a very young age.
- There is the risk of not finishing (secondary) school.
- It will leave you feeling guilty and worthless. You may not find trust again. People may not trust you again.

- You may also be at risk of becoming unfaithful to your husband, if you get married. If you can't control yourself before marriage, will you be able to afterwards?

Today, technology and fashion designers are encouraging people to dress scantily and to have sex. If you look at the films, magazines, journals and adverts, you will see half-naked women all around. You see artists and models dressing like idols to seduce men into sex. All these are deviations from the truth. That is not how it is meant to be. Your nakedness is meant to be covered, respected and protected, not exposed and insulted.

The modern cultures also encourage youth to have sex using a condom. While condoms reduce the chances of users acquiring STD's or becoming pregnant, they are not 100% safe. They can leak or break, permitting viruses or semen to flow through them. As far as plastic is concerned, condoms may have tiny holes that can be measured in nanometers and can permit the flow of very tiny viruses into your system. Although proper and consistent condom use may prevent the transmission of other sexually transmitted infections, I want you to be 100% safe, and the only way to **total safety is total abstinence**. I want you to run away from sexual relationships because it is a sin against your body and against God. It was God who created our sex organs; he makes them develop and mature with time, but he has set the best time for sex and that is inside marriage. As I'll explain, the Bible is clear that any sex outside marriage is sin.

Biblical Principles

The Bible is clear on this point and warns us to abstain from sexual sin.

> It's God's will that you should be sanctified: that you should avoid sexual immorality; that each of you should learn to

control his own body in a way that is honorable, not in passionate lust like the heathen, who do not know God.

—1 Thessalonians 4:3-5

Put to death, therefore, whatever belongs to your earthly nature: sexual immorality, impurity, lust, evil desires and greed, which is idolatry. Because of these things the wrath of God is coming.

—Colossians 3:5-6

The body is not meant for sexual immorality but for the Lord and the Lord for the body. . . Do you not know that your bodies are members of Christ himself? . . . Flee from sexual immorality. All other sins a man commits are outside his body, but he who sins sexually sins against his own body. Do you not know that your body is the temple of the Holy Spirit, who is in you, whom you have received from God? You are not your own; you were bought at a price. Therefore honor God with your body.

—1 Corinthians 6:13-19

Be careful then my sister, because even those who think they can't fall in this matter have crashed. This is not because they weren't careful, but because they may have acted naively some times.

In 2 Samuel 13:1-22 you will find the story of how Amnon raped his half-sister Tamar. Even today, the Devil is still using men to play similar tricks on young innocent girls, just to destroy their bright future. Many of these girls have entered into rooms meant for men without the thought of harm, but ended up being molested and disdained. Therefore, never go into any room or stay in any room meant for boys or with boys alone. Men are stronger than women; they can force girls into doing what they don't want to do. If you must go into a boys room or in a room where there are boys, (that is if it becomes a must) then don't agree to enter alone. But you know, it can never be a must. Don't be deceived by invitations like, "Come and cook for me," or "Come and get something in my room or in my friend's room," or even an invitation for meeting in a dark place. Don't agree! No matter how good or innocent the person may seem, people can change overnight. The Devil can pretend to be a good person only to bite like a cobra.

Wise Conduct

I must be frank with you; your own emotions may betray you. You might actually be the one who will desire someone to hold you or touch you. Some guys may even attempt to get to you through your trusted friends, and such friends may also betray you by agreeing to accompany you to some of the places I've advised you not to go to, then betray you by running away. When such happens, don't wait there for a second more. If you don't want to regret and cry, then **RUN** for your own good. Why must things be done in secret? If there is truth in it let it be done in the light.

Also, do not accept gifts from strangers. Sometimes, these gifts can be charmed and, unless you're a strong believer in Christ Jesus, they may affect you. We'll talk about becoming a Christian later on.

I am not saying you should not have boys as friends, or not to accept gifts from known and trusted people (although they too can change). What I am saying is that you should be extra careful; be wise and sensitive in your dealings with people. Watch the kind of things you discuss with them, the kind of jokes you play with them, the kind of places you meet or go to with them, and the kind of activities or plays you are involved in with them. Do not go after favor and gifts from them because some may request a pay back.

The Bible teaches us to be as wise as snakes and as harmless as doves. I may not have informed you about all the tricks the devil uses to lure teenage girls into sexual sin, because I'm a human, and I'm limited. However this is what I believe; if you fear God and are careful to run away from trouble, being open to respectable older ones and teachers, if you are careful to do what is right wherever you are, God will help you recognize unwise behaviors and provide a way to escape temptation and the attacks of the devil (1 Cor. 10:13).

To stand is not usually easy. This I know very well myself as a woman. As the temptations come, you will find some inviting, and you will find it increasingly hard to cope, but it is only those who endure to the end will be saved. For choosing to do what is right, others may insult you, call you names like 'fool, small girl, bush girl, mummy's pet,' etc. just to humiliate you. Let me encourage you. There are those who have stayed victorious over peer pressure and who are heroines today. Others, despite making slight mistakes, have braced up and determined to continue with life in the right way, not accepting defeat as final. Today, they are all glad they have done so.

> No temptation has seized you except what is common to man. And God is faithful; He will not let you be tempted beyond what you can bear. But when you are tempted, He will also provide a way out so that you can stand up under it.
>
> —1 Corinthians 10:13

"For though a righteous man falls seven times, he rises again..." (Proverbs 24:16). If you are willing, determined and obedient, that is when you will eat and enjoy the sweet fruits of life. Here is a trustworthy saying James 1:2-4:

> Consider it a sheer gift, friends, when tests and challenges come at you from all sides. You know that under pressure, your faith-life is forced into the open and shows its true colors. So don't try to get out of anything prematurely. Let it do its work so you become mature and well-developed, not deficient in any way.

As much as I've advised you to run from sex because of the negative outcomes, above all else resist sexual temptation because you love God, because you do not want to make Him sad, because you also do not want to disappoint those of us who love and care about you.

Discussion Points

1. What would you say are the main reasons teen girls fall into sexual temptations?
2. What personal reasons would stop you from sexual sin?
3. Discuss the issue of boyfriend and girlfriend among teens today (its spread and effects).
4. What Bible passages talk about keeping our selves pure from sexual sin?
5. Discuss the contribution models and fashion designers make to the development of teens; would you describe these as being positive or negative?
6. What safeguards could you put into place in your own life that will protect you from falling prey to those who wish to take advantage of you?

CHAPTER 3

TEEN FEVERS

"You never get to be a teenage twice, please listen to me" Malik's father said to his son as the angry boy dashed out of the house slamming the door behind him. The cause of the argument was that his parents had been trying to tell him things about being a teenager, which he, Malik, considered insulting and prying into his privacy. The angry young man went to his friend's house and began expressing his displeasure about his parents pestering him.

> I'm fifteen, for heaven's sake, yet my parents treat me like I'm some sort of ten year old. You are lucky your parents don't treat you like mine treat me.

Thomas answered, "Well not exactly, my parents also try to teach me stuff too." "At least not in the way mine do," Malik interjected. In the middle of their chat, Malik asked his friend "Have you any idea what 'never being a teenager twice' could mean?" "Why ask that?" Thomas asked in return. "That was the thing I heard my Dad say to me as I left the house today." "I don't know, but we could ask my Dad." Malik didn't like the idea, but Thomas insisted that they wouldn't disclose where the statement came from. So both friends approached Thomas' Dad and asked him the question. To this, the older man said,

> We always compare teenagers to people lined up in canoes, each in their own. They are in control of these canoes and are on a voyage across a sea they have never crossed before. They can only cross it once in a life time.

He continued by explaining that once the teenager outgrows his years of being a teenager, he or she can only look back at the things he has done and cannot undo them. Malik then asked, "Why do some parents keep trying to teach their children everything?" hoping not to expose their agreement. Yet, he didn't need to, because the old man already knew of the troubled youth's situation, so he answered saying,

> You see, every parent see their child as one of these very many, new, inexperienced voyagers across the sea of teenage life. Many have made it before you; many more shall come after you. However, some who have come to this stage did not make it safely across, while others did not make it at all. They drowned and were lost at sea, mostly because they were careless, or refused to listen to the guides and advice they were given. Then, when they have capsized, they never get to relive their teenage years again.
>
> So my young friend, don't be angry when we try in many ways to help you. We do not want you to make the mistakes many of us made when we were young. We only offer you all that we do out of the love and care which we have for you and for your future.

Both boys thanked him and Malik asked his friend to accompany him home, "I need to apologize to my father," he said, as both friends headed home.

You see, the teenage life is a stage full of excitement and fun. There are many things to discover and there are many things to learn from. Those who make wise choices and decisions and take wise, firm and bold steps are the ones who always end up on the best shores at the end of the voyage. Those who discover and put into practice their talents, strengths and special abilities are the ones who end up with colorful lives. These we pray you will have. Remember, as assuring as this stage can be, it can also be dangerous. You must pay attention.

Growth takes place from stage to stage. Children grow from infancy; learning to sit, crawl, stand, walk, talk, run, etc. and that is exactly how teens are. They become like babies in the adult world. They begin to learn how to think, speak and behave like adults.

Another thing we have noticed is that when babies are born, they become exposed to many diseases like measles, polio, scarlet fever, yellow fever, chickenpox, hepatitis, meningitis, etc. Whether they are born in rich or poor families, when they contract a disease, they suffer greatly and may die. The remedy however, is immunization or proper treatment. In a similar way, we have noticed that teenagers also have their own type of disease, which may attack them as well since they too are also like babies in the adult world. Although teenage diseases are not physical, like those we listed above, they have led many to psychiatric hospitals, prisons, medical hospitals and even down to the grave, regardless of whether the teenager is rich or poor. The only safety measure is to be immunized against these terrible teenage palavers, or to ensure proper and complete treatment when already contracted.

We want to tell you more about the most dangerous ones. We call them the four teenage fevers.

Anxiety Fever

Philosophers and psychologists have tried in many ways to define or explain anxiety. Anxiety can be explained as a state of uneasiness of the mind. It is an overwhelming feeling of dissatisfaction and restlessness where nothing seems to be right. It pushes you to think and act fast through situations. Anxiety can lead to fear and depression. Anxiety can simply be referred to as that type of feeling you have when you are called to say or do something before people. You feel nervous and uneasy at times; your body starts to tremble and your heart starts to beat fast. That is anxiety.

When a girl becomes a teenager, she becomes more exposed to anxiety. This is because at this stage, there are a lot of choices and decisions she'll have to make; issues such as what to study, the type of lifestyle to live, where to study, how to relate with others, etc. Before long, such issues can make her develop fear and confusion about what to do. The teenager has just begun to engage her mind in decision making which is a scary process.

We call this a teenage fever because when a teenager gets caught by anxiety and is confused and challenged by uncertainty, he or she'll hardly calm down to think or reason. This has led many to quick, but wrong lifestyle choices and has thus affected them badly. At this stage, their minds are set to quick thinking to get what they want. Nothing will please them unless they are doing what they have purposed to do. Whatever will lead someone to destruction is what we call a disease.

Let's explain this fever a little further for you. Some of the things that can show you that a teenager is likely having this fever might include the following:

- she might begin to think she is being underestimated by peers or older ones;
- she might always want to do things her way;
- she might begin to feel as if she is not given enough freedom to express herself as she wants;
- she may begin to devise or initiate ways of doing what she feels like doing;

- she may want to copy or imitate celebrities or superstars at whatever cost without considering the implications or consequences.

Such affected victims may find it hard to accept advice or warning from anyone.

Let's give you a typical example of anxiety fever.

We want to also let you know that most teenage anxiety cases relate to issue of body image, insecurities, comparison, and fear of performance.

Daisy was overweight, so kids at school called her "Biggy" and other were so mean they called her "Piggy." She desired to join the dance club but was afraid she would not be able to do well. Sometimes, Daisy would start getting set for school but when she gets to wear her uniform and sees how "big" she is for the uniform she fake being sick just to remain at home where she won't be mocked. Because she has been continually pick upon in school Daisy developed a fear of being attacked anywhere she is. She felt since she was fat and not pretty, no one liked her. This made her keep to herself mostly and had no friends. Sometimes at home, Daisy would lock herself in her room and cry.

One day at church their youth pastor preached from the book of Psalm 139:14. The pastor said God created us all in his image, and that we are individually unique to him. He said a lot of things that served to brighten up Daisy's heart. On their way home from church, Daisy couldn't wait to get home before she asked her parents, "Is it true that we are special however we look?" Her parents were surprised at their daughter's question. So they asked her in return, "Why?" She said, "Well, our pastor said so in church today." Her Dad answered, "Yes dear we are each special before God." "If so" Daisy continued "why do some kids in school call me names and make me feel bad?" "Oh dear so sorry about that" her parents responded.

Later that evening while they ate dinner, Daisy's mother said to her,

> People often insult what they don't understand, and others call you names because they cannot be like you. Like the pastor told you today, whenever they call you names always remember that you are special.

She continued by saying

> It will not be enough to just feel special, you should also try your best to be good at what you like to do because that will make them respect you and stop calling you names.

Her Dad added by saying "Regardless of what others think of you or call you, always remember that before God and to us, you are special."

Daisy's new-found knowledge helped to build her self-esteem and cope with the pressures in school. It didn't happen at once, but gradually she was able to resist the urge of feeling unloved or of not being special.

To cut the long story short, as Daisy grew she also lost the weight and was very happy that she learnt from her parents and her pastor at church.

Take note that not everyone who suffers from anxiety always have the opportunity that Daisy had. You reading this have double privileges to learn, use it well. Some due to anxiety have resolved to fight back and act in ways that are not acceptable. Some anxious teens who do not get help become depressed, and this has led many to commit terrible crimes and even suicide.

Anxiety is a common problem among teenagers. We are sure you are already seeing some people behaving in a similar way. When you begin to feel like Daisy, or if you observe anyone acting similar to her below are some lessons we want you to think about and apply them as remedies whenever you are getting anxious:

- **<u>We are all uniquely created:</u>** What many fail to understand is that we were created differently for different reasons. And, since we didn't create ourselves, we ought to accept our nature the way we are. This doesn't mean we should live carelessly. God expects us to take good care of our bodies. About being obese (being fat, chubby or plump) however, sometimes this results from lack of exercise, the types of food we eat and sometimes it can be hereditary. There are many resources online that can help you live healthily, you can check them out to see which helps you most.

- **<u>Be positive:</u>** Rather than dwell on what you do not have, or what others say you are or you are not, think about what you have and be happy for it. There are quite a lot of people who were insulted as either being fat, nerds, freaks, not smart, poor or weak. However, some of such people instead of feeling sorry for themselves, looked deep and discovered something special about themselves, which made those who insulted them to respect them afterwards.

- **<u>Patience:</u>** A man in a hurry always misses the way (Proverbs 19:2). There is a time for everything (Ecclesiastes 3:2). "Seek your happiness in the Lord, and He will give you your heart's desires. . . . Wait for the Lord and keep his ways (patiently) and He will exalt you." (Psalms 37:4, 34). Be patient as you grow. Daisy had to learn to be patient with her weight, as time passed she lost it without effort. However, like her parents said to her, being fat doesn't mean one is ugly, as we are all special before God our Creator.

- **<u>Respect:</u>** Passages like 1 Peter 5:5 and Ephesians 6:1 tell us to obey our parents. Yet, this doesn't limit respect to our parents alone or elderly ones alone. We should respect everyone. Respect means having regard or courtesy for someone or something. Hence, you should respect your peers and even those younger than you are, respect your body, your life and the privilege you have to learn this.

When you show respect, in most cases you get respect for you in return.

When you are able to take care of anxiety, you will discover like Daisy did that you are special, and that God has something special that only you can do so well. You will also discover peace of mind and find purpose. Therefore, when you feel anxious always remember the story of Daisy who almost gave up but overcame.

Anger Fever

Obviously, the major disorders teenagers face have to do with their emotions. Anger (to become angry) is an emotional problem many teenagers face, and many have been unable to handle it. As a result, they have gotten into serious trouble. Anger is a problem everyone has, even adults. It means to have strong feelings when something has happened or if someone did or said something which the one who is angry thinks is bad. Since all of us get angry at particular things and moments, the only way is to control it. If a teenager learns this, she stands a better chance of controlling or managing it as an adult.

We read in a book titled, *"Today's Heroes,"* the story of Dr. Ben Carson and how he struggled with anger as a teenager. From his story, there are some lessons teenagers should learn particularly about anger. The story goes thus:

When Dr. Ben Carson was still a teenager, his mother brought him clothes (trousers) but he refused them saying he did not like them. His mother had worked hard to get money and order them, but Ben wanted to look like his friends. His mother had begged him, "Bennie, we don't always get what we want." Ben was already angry with his mother and he became angrier. He screamed at her and said, "I will," and he swung his arm angrily at her. If not for Curtis, his brother, who caught him and wrestled him away, he would have hit his mother. Even then, Ben did not recognize he had anger fever. He just felt he was being himself.

At school, Ben often got into trouble because he could not control his anger. Sometimes he hit his friends and injured them badly. There was a time he was even taken to the principal because he had hurt someone badly. One day, however, something happened that brought Ben back to his senses. He and his friend were listening to the radio at his friend Bob's house. Bob changed the station and Ben changed it back. Bob still changed it again. This got Ben angry and he grabbed the camping knife in his pocket, snapped the blade open and plunged at Bob's stomach. Ben was lucky the blade had hit Bob's large metal belt buckle. Bob was so scared he looked at Ben in fear and surprise and could not say anything. Ben felt ashamed at his reaction and thankful to God that he had not killed his friend; he would have ended his life in prison. That day, Ben went home and cried. He prayed to God and read the Bible.

He prayed for God to change him because he realized that his anger had become a problem. That was when he realized that he actually had the anger fever. Then he read Proverbs 16:32, which says, "A man who controls his temper is better than one who takes a city." It was as if God were talking to him. After that episode in their small bathroom, his body stopped shaking and he stopped crying. He felt a new sense of peace fill his heart. He had been in the bathroom for four hours. After that, God kept helping him control his temper and he never had problems again with his anger.

Anger is not only limited to teen boys; girls also have anger problems too. Gift was a girl who also struggled with anger during her teenage years. Her sibling would usually tease her when she is angry saying that because she is angry the clouds will gather and it will rain.

When anything happens which she does not like, she will shout at the person who did it and even abuse the person.

One day Gift returned from school hungry, but only to discover that there was no lunch for her. She got so angry and started to shout "Mummy! Mummy! I am hungry." Her mother was sympathetic and said gently to Gift,

> Some children came and helped me do some work in the house
> so when they finished I served them the food that was in the
> house but…

Before she could finish the statement Gift walked out on her mother, angrily banging the door shut behind her. She went to her room and began to cry. Little did she know that her mum had sent her elder brother to buy her snacks from a nearby eatery, while she waited for the food her mother was cooking to be ready. Gift's mother went after her to her room because she had previously been talking to her about her anger, telling her to be careful so she doesn't get into trouble. On getting to her room, she found Gift angrily talking to herself. "Honey," her mother began but Gift shouted back at her "Don't talk to me, I am hungry." Her mummy patiently started again saying, "You should have listened to what I have to say, I was trying to tell you that…"

> Mummy I don't care since you have given all the food to the
> children and then we will remain hungry, I'm going out to get
> snacks for myself,

Gift retorted disrespectfully at her mother. "Now will you shut up and listen to me you stubborn girl?" Gift's mother shouted angrily back at her. Then, Gift's brother returned with the snack and came over to the room with it in his hands. "What is happening?" he enquired. Gifts mother said, "This is what I was trying to tell you and your stubborn mouth will not let you listen," and walked out of the room. Her brother said to her "If you don't learn to control your anger you will miss a blessing one day." He said that and dropped the snack on her bed and left. Then Gift started to cry. She knelt down by her bed, prayed to God, and said "Please God help me, this anger is leading me into trouble and disrespecting my mother. Please, help me to stop being angry." She prayed and cried there for a while then went to her mother and knelt down apologizing for her character. Her mother forgave her and told her not to let anger control her but that she should learn to control it.

Today, Gift is a married woman and she teaches teenage girls in her church. She has always used her life story to teach teenager how anger had led her into fights at school and into disrespecting her teachers and parents and other things she did not want to do. We are sure that some of the things Gift would teach her teenagers will be the same as we shall share with you.

Anger is normal, but our reaction, or how we use it, is what matters most. When you get angry, do not entertain thoughts like;

- "It is not my fault"
- "They are bad/evil"

Here is some we found helpful:

- Don't make decisions when you are angry. Give yourself time to calm down.
- Don't act in aggression, impulsively or violently.
- Don't be passive by keeping anger inside of you. All these will only give negative results. You may begin to feel like a victim nursing wounds (malice, resentment) and this can lead you to depression.
- When you get angry, some healthy attitudes to display may include:
- Admit you are angry and you ought to control it. Tell yourself, "I'm responsible for my reactions." It is not so much what others do that

makes you angry. You either get angry or you don't, and that is entirely your responsibility.

- Consider how you can harness your anger to get stronger, smarter and safer from whatever is angering you.
- Explore the roots of where your anger is coming from. Have your rights been violated in some way? Is someone not treating you properly or with the respect deserved? Or are you selfishly wanting your own way? Deal appropriately with what you recognize as the source.
- You can also choose to
- Pray in your heart, asking God for direction.
- Take powerful effective actions to make things better. Perhaps you could approach the one who has made you angry and try to make peace.
- Forgive immediately. When you are hurt, forgive immediately.

These are just a few of the very many clues to effective anger management. We're just beginning to learn to use them ourselves. If we'd known and used them earlier, we would have mastered them by now. You are getting to know them now; master them and you shall sail through your teenage years with much ease. You can also be rest assured of a nice adulthood.

If you are already struggling with anger, you can do like Ben did. Admit it first. That is the number one way to cure this teenage fever.

Depression Fever

We want to share with you the story of Simi. Simi grew in a poor home. Her father died when she was still a baby, and her mother had to raise the three of them in a little house. Their mother was not an educated woman so she had difficulties getting a well-paid job. Nevertheless, she sold a few provisions on the table to be able to provide food for them all and to train them in school. Gradually, Mummy Simi's business grew and she was able to pay for her two sons to attend secondary school. When it was Simi's turn, she also was able to get admission into a day secondary school at the age of 12.

All the while Simi had been nursing the desire to have the kind of clothes others wore. Girls of her age wore the latest clothes, while all she had were used clothes and shoes that her mother was able to buy for them. Because of this, Simi started a business of her own to get money. She began selling sachet water where her mother sold her things. She was able to get some money but not as much as she wanted, so eventually she stopped altogether.

Furthermore, Simi had a boy who was her good friend. He went to their house, they did assignments together and she liked him. But then he started to go to another of her friends who wore better clothes than Simi. So Simi thought that he had left her because she was poor. This made her feel very bad about herself, her family and everything around her. Without her knowledge, the feelings she carried in her mind made her not want to have any friends in school, and she kept away from people. She was always sad and her grades gradually dropped and dropped.

When Simi's mother observed that Simi was becoming quieter and was not having friends to visit her and she was not visiting any of her friends, she prayed to God for wisdom on how to help her daughter. Then one day, she saved some money and bought Simi a beautiful dress. Simi was so excited that she jumped and hugged her mother repeatedly thanking her over and over again. Then Simi's mother sat her down and told her,

> I noticed that you were depressed my daughter and I was not
> happy about it. I want you to be happy with what you have.

> Someday God is going to provide more for us, but until you
> are happy with the little you already have, many more good
> things that will make you happy may not come your way:
> remember that it is God who gives good things. So please don't
> be depressed but be content with what you have.

Simi was so happy with her mother. After a little while her grades in school improved, and she resumed her business. It also grew and she was able to help her mother from the profits she made from her sales after school. When Simi completed her JSS class, she was ready to go into a boarding school, and she told her mother,

> Thank you for teaching me this good lesson Mummy. By the
> grace of God I will not be depressed again. I will be happy with
> what I have.

Simi was able to complete her secondary school as the best student of her time and got a scholarship to study in the United States of America.

Jesus provided a guide towards living a depressed free life when he said:

> Therefore, I tell you, do not worry about life, what you will eat
> or drink; or about your body, what you will wear. Is not life
> more important than food, and the body more important than
> clothes? Look at the birds of the air; they do not sow or reap or
> store away in barns, and yet your heavenly Father feeds them.
> Are you not much more valuable than they? Which of you by
> worrying can add a single hour to his life? And why do you
> worry about clothes? See how the lilies of the field grow. They
> do not labor or spin. Yet I tell you that not even Solomon, in all
> his splendor, was dressed like one of these. If that is how God
> clothes the grass of the field, which is here today and tomorrow
> is thrown into the fire, will he not much more clothe you, O
> you of little faith? So do not worry, saying, "What shall we
> eat?" or "What shall we drink?" or "what shall we wear?" For

the pagans run after all these things, and your heavenly father knows that you need them. But seek first his kingdom and his righteousness, and all these things will be given to you as well. Therefore, do not worry about tomorrow, for tomorrow will worry about itself. Each day has enough trouble of its own.

—Matthew 6:25-34

Going by Jesus' command not to worry, Simi would have been saved from experiencing a lot of stress she went through. Now that she is determined to live free of depression, she is simply trying to follow in Jesus' footstep on not worrying about things of this life. Do you know that some (especially girls your age and above) worry so much about their outward appearances? Some don't like their body shapes, their hair, their faces and many other things about themselves. This has often led quite a lot to serious problems of the mind that may require help. To put it simply, depression is the state of feeling lonely, unable, rejected, sad and unwanted. It can show on the faces of the depressed and even in their actions, though some are good at hiding it. Sometimes, when disappointed, you may notice people looking dull, not lively, or slow. Some may also display anger. That is a simple picture of a depressed person. Some causes of depression among teenagers might include:

- **Unappreciated Efforts:** When someone does a good thing but no one seems to notice or say "Well done," it may lead to depression. We have seen teenagers destroy the things they have created because their efforts have not been appreciated.

- **Dissatisfaction:** When teenagers are not satisfied with themselves; their performance at school or at home, they may get depressed. When they cannot get another person satisfied – a parent, teacher or a close friend – they get depressed. They start to get the feelings of, "I cannot do anything right." Also when they can't attain the target they have set such as, getting a new shirt, a pair of shoes, a type of game, etc, they get sad and depressed.

- **<u>Envy:</u>** A teenager can become depressed simply because others own something and they don't have it.

- **<u>Medical or Psychological Imbalance:</u>** Furthermore, depression is not just feeling sad and discouraged. Being temporarily sad about a situation does not really mean that a person is depressed. Everyone goes through a moment of sadness and displeasure. However, the thing with depression is that sometimes there is a physical imbalance in the brain requiring medical treatment – at least for a short time to reset the brain. Other times there are deep-rooted spiritual, emotional or physiological problems that grow and take root gradually in the mind of the person. That is why depression often takes time and sometimes require spiritual and psychological counselling from qualified counsellors, psychologist or even psychiatrists.

This becomes a fever because, when a teenager becomes depressed, she will not perform well in anything at all. It could also lead to illnesses.

We know very well that this is a problem that you may very well face. Your mood will be flipping and changing, because of the fluctuating hormones we have already discussed. Always remember never to allow yourself to be imprisoned by this fever. Understand that looking sad is not good. It is a fever. It will affect your performance. It is a trap meant to drag you back. Many who have allowed depression to control them for so long are regretting it today. They wish they had just cheered up and carried on with what they needed to have done.

If this disease catches up with you, we'll suggest you use some of the following remedies:

- Pray and tell God your problem.

- Remember being sad or angry is not good for you.
- Being depressed will only slow you down.
- It steals away your time.
- "The joy of the Lord is your strength" (Nehemiah 8:10).
- Always avoid depression. Even adults suffer from it today and it could result in hypertension.

If you, as a teenager, are able to learn to treat this fever, your adulthood will be less stressful. For more help,

- Don't keep malice towards someone in your heart
- Be content and happy with what you have.
- Don't envy others. It is a sin to do so. (1 Timothy 6:6)
- Don't worry if others don't appreciate or compliment you. God notices and cares about you.
- Don't worry if you don't have clothes or shoes. If you worry, it will lead you to sin. (Matthew 6:25-34).

As you read this, we want you to look around. We're sure you will see practical examples amongst your friends and others as well. We're taking this time to inform you so that you can be a doctor to your friends who might be suffering from any of these teenage fevers. There are moments you might feel sad. At some point, everyone feels down, but it becomes a problem when such feelings continue for long periods of time.

Fear Fever

We are sure that you already have an idea of fear, meaning being or becoming afraid, due to some danger or the possibility of something bad occurring. We hope as we explain it you will be able to have a wider picture of what it means and how it could affect you as a teenager (since it is a fever).

Like anger, depression and anxiety, fear is also a feeling that builds up from inside a person. We want you to know that this fear fever can be of two forms; that is why we will give you two illustrations to help you.

The first is about a guy called Dathan. You see, Dathan believed very much that he has talents in him. However, despite his knowledge of this truth and even confirmation he gets from other people (because he was always being told "Boy, you are talented"), he couldn't explain why, for so long, he could not do what he longed to do in his heart. He dreamed of singing in large concerts and of writing great books, yet he was not able to start, even at a small level. You see, in as much as he knew he had what it would take and he had the desire, there was a wicked enemy that had kept him imprisoned for so long. That enemy is the fever called fear. He was afraid people would look down on him. He was afraid he was going to make mistakes if he tried. He was afraid of so many things. As a result, opportunities came and passed him by all the time. The worst thing was he did not know that he was sick with the fear fever.

The second example we have for you is that of a girl called Blessing. Blessing had friends whom she had just met in school, Rose and Kauna. Rose and Kauna were already friends at home, so Blessing became the third. They were all in the same class. Within a short period of time the three became very close. Soon, exams came. However, all the times Blessing told the others to come for preps, they would refuse. Instead, Rose and Kauna told Blessing that she was going to sit between them so that they could copy her work. Blessing knew it was wrong to cheat during exams. She knew that if she did it, she would be disrespecting her parents, teachers and even God who said we should obey rules and not cheat or steal. She told them all these but they said it was not cheating or stealing but it was just helping. They also threatened that if she wasn't willing, they'd stop being her friends. Blessing became afraid. She knew that if Rose and Kauna were not her friends, they would insult her and say bad things to her. So, because of the fear of being ridiculed, insulted and humiliated, she accepted.

At home, the three became like three inseparable cords. Before long, Rose invited them to her birthday party. After that, Blessing got to find out that the other two had boyfriends they were sleeping with and they introduced her to one called George. Blessing's heart was pounding hard in her chest; she knew clearly what it meant to sleep with a boy and she rejected and said no. Rose and Kauna begged her. When she stood her ground, they threatened to send her out and never to talk with her again. Since that was her fear, she gave in.

One day, she got sick and she suspected she was pregnant because she had missed her period. The thought of being pregnant in SS2 scared her more. To Blessing's terror, the result was positive. She became frantic, afraid, confused and cried. Her friends assured her it was all right, that they had experienced it but they had come through. Blessing was so afraid and was willing to do anything to stop her parents from knowing about it. However, her friends' advice was to abort it. Again, Blessing was driven into a more agonizing state of fear. She knew what it meant. It simply meant murder, destroying another life and it was sin. She cried and cried, wanting an alternative solution. The girls said it was either she took their advice or she should leave. Blessing could not face the fear of telling her parents and, still afraid, she believed their threats.

After swallowing some pills they gave her, she immediately began to scream, holding her stomach and fell to the ground and passed out. She opened her eyes to realize that she had been in the hospital for two days unconscious. When she opened her eyes, her mother thanked God but began to cry. *She knew*, Blessing thought. She felt terribly bad and began to cry too. Her mother took care of her until she regained her health.

She recovered from the sickness but not without consequences. Her friends got expelled from school, were taken to the police station and charged to court. She was also expelled from school. Above all, the worst news from the doctor, news no young woman in her right senses would want to hear was, "She may not be able to bear children again because her womb has been affected by the drugs she took." Fear fever robbed Blessing of her valuable future. This is just one of the many examples of people who have been destroyed by this slow poison (a green snake under green grass) called fear.

Fear fever has two ways of crippling a teenager. One – like in our story – it keeps you imprisoned. You can't express your gifts and exercise your talents. Two, it can – like in Blessing's story – keep you from refusing or avoiding things that are bad, leading you from one level to another until it has destroyed you completely, leaving no trace of the "you" that you were before or the "you" that you dream to be in future.

The only fear that is good is the fear of God. This does not mean being afraid of God. Rather, it means reverencing God to the point that you refuse to do bad things because doing them will not make God happy. This is healthy fear because it will save you from danger and self-destruction. That is the type of fear Blessing should have practiced, not the fear of people or things. It is the devil who makes us scared of saying *"NO" to sin and bad habits*. It is him who makes us timid and fearful. God said he has not given us the spirit of fear and timidity; instead, he has given us the spirit of power, of love and of self-discipline (2 Timothy 1:7).

You will face fears too. Since Adam and Eve sinned in the Garden of Eden, they ran and hid because they were afraid. Fear has since become a part of human beings. We are afraid of the dark, we are afraid of making wrong choices and decisions, we are afraid of failure, we are afraid of the unseen things. Fear is everywhere.

However, we are not left helpless. God has provided ways to be victorious. As a teenager, you can be cured and control this fever through some of the following ways:

- **Being Bold:** This is the key to freedom from the prison of timidity and fear. It is the secret Blessing should have used. Don't be intimidated. Always be confident, bold and courageous (Joshua 1:6-9).

- **Don't Fear Making Mistakes:** When you are called to do a thing or when you want to try something, remind yourself that "no one is perfect." We all make mistakes. Unless we make mistakes, we cannot learn and improve.

- **Think Positive Thoughts:** When you think of failure and fear, they will control you and will make you act and behave negatively.

This list of four fevers is not exclusive of the problems that make teenagers fail in their sail across this new sea of experience. However, we are sure if you are able to train yourself to handle and tackle these four, the rest will be easier for you to handle. Do not fail to learn; read more about issues that relate to you and your surroundings. By so doing, you will become wiser among your peers.

- **Ultimately Trusting in God:** Trusting God to be in control of every situation and give us the wisdom and strength we need to overcome the situation.

Discussion Points

1. Which of the teenage fevers do you think are most prevalent around you?
2. How can you describe the effects of these fevers on the teens in your school and your surrounding environment? Would you say its increasing or decreasing?
3. Have you at some points been challenged by any of the discussed teenage fevers? How did you handle it? And how differently would you handle such when faced with it now?

CHAPTER 4

FRIENDS

There is the story of a very famous leader who, when asked in an interview if he had friends, replied that he has. When asked to name them he said his best friend is his childhood friend Abraham. He was further asked how he became friends with his not so famous childhood friend. Then he told a short story;

Growing up I was quiet and shy. My father was a factory worker and my mother was a cleaner. With them not being around most of the time I was left at home with my two younger siblings. Abraham's parents just moved into the neighbourhood and he was soon enrolled into school. Most of the kids were in school but I wasn't.

One day Abraham came over to our front yard where I always played alone and asked me what my name was. I reluctantly told him and he asked if we could be friends. Not knowing what else to say I said, "Yes." From that moment on Abraham would always come to our house after school to play. We would play around the streets and the neighbourhood till our parents were back. As we became fond of each other, he began to teach me the things he learnt in school. As simple as this was it formed the foundation of my formal education. By the time I was twelve I enrolled in school without my parents' knowledge. When they later found out they didn't try to stop me. We worked with Abraham in people's yards and all petty works we could to save for my tuition. He didn't need to, because his parents paid his, but he was always there to help me.

Well, from there, we continued to become closer. Till today, I am always grateful to this friend who has become closer than a brother. God used him to set me on the path to greatness. That's the story of my one true friend.

In your new level, the most common advice you will receive from many people is; **choose your friends wisely.** We are also joining them to say the same thing to you. It is the most emphasized advice, yet it is often the most neglected. The effect caused by the neglect of this single and simple advice lasts a very long time, sometimes for an entire lifetime.

Friendship is a relationship between two or more people based on mutual trust, love and approval characterized by a genuine tendency to assist, support and care for one another. You will have close friends, casual friends, and acquaintances. The issue is this: we all need friends because friendship is very important, because:

- It provides companionship and individual motivation.
- It provides an avenue for problem-sharing and problem solving.
- It provides opportunity for better choice of future marriage partners.
- It promotes self-esteem and builds self-confidence.

If friendship is important, what kind of friends will you need to get you to achieve the above listed reasons? We want to let you know that there **are good** friends and **bad friends.**

Some qualities of good friends may include (but are not limited to) the following:

- Trustworthiness; they believe in you.

- Respect; they have regard for you and your opinion.
- Reliability; they can be depended upon at all times
- Confidentiality; they keep your secrets.
- Supportive; they are ready to stand by you in good and bad times.
- Tolerance; they are ready to forgive you when you offend them.
- Honesty; they tell you the truth always, even when it hurts.
- Commonality; you share the same interest, attitudes and values.
- Sacrificial; they are always ready to go an extra mile with you and for you.
- Cooperation; they are willing to assist you and offer help whenever you need it.
- Motivation; they encourage you to achieve your goals in life.

Bad friends on the other hand are uncaring, unloving, dishonest, ungodly, impatient, proud, deceptive, intolerant, unforgiving and selfish. They will always want to control you. They are not even fit to be called friends.

At home, at school, church and on the internet, you will meet many acquaintances. Some may become casual friends, but be very observant and careful of those you take in as close friends. Such have the power to either "make you" into who you were created to be, or to "break you" away from what God wants for you.

Many choose friends for different reasons but our advice for you is not to have too many friends. Having friends is not all about having many people you know and move with. That is just being in the crowd. "A man of many companions may come to ruin" (Proverbs 18:24).

Never choose friends because of what they have materially. It is better to have a poor friend who loves you, than to be with a rich person who looks down on you. Those who have hidden or open bad characters should not be your friends because bad company corrupts good morals (1Corinthians 15:33). Do not let yourself feel imprisoned by a friend whom you suddenly discover has a bad lifestyle. It is better to break free and be safe, than to continue in that path to a terrible ending. Dear, if you stay with the wise, you will become wise, but staying with the foolish will make you foolish too (Proverbs 13:20). The type of friends you mix up with today will determine the type of future you are preparing for yourself tomorrow.

We have understood some values of friendship and we want to share them with you. We have our problems, but we have come to know that true friendship is the type that agrees on issues, settles quarrels, and always determines to make things right. That is why we are best of friends today, and are working together for a common goal.

The good and bad friends will come to you (you can be rest assured that the bad will come first). Please, if your friendship is not making you increase and improve academically and in your knowledge of God, run from it. Good friends are hard to find, but they are there. Do your best to be someone's good friend. Work to be that good friend others will be searching for.

Discussion Points

1. How many friends do you have?
2. How many of them can you say are true friends that fit the description of a true friend in this chapter?
3. Discuss some of the positive thing you have learnt from your friend.
4. Discuss the friends-making networks around you such as Facebook, Snapchat, Instagram, WhatsApp BBM, Qzone, Twitter, ebuddy, YouTube, Yahoo, Google, Skype, Viber, LinkedIn, Telegram, Badoo, Myspace and all other social media.
5. With the friends-making methods available today would you say making true friends is being made easy or hard?
6. Using the friendship of David and Jonathan found in 1 Samuel 20:1-42, what is the Bible teaching about true friendship?

CHAPTER 5

CAREER CHOICE

"I want to be a farmer," Amina said and the whole class started to laugh at her. Some started to make jest of her, jeering and calling her, "Farmer Amina." Others called her "Amina the farmer." Teacher John, Amina's class teacher, asked the class to be quiet and said to Amina, "That is a very interesting thing for a girl to do. Amina, can you tell us why you want to be a farmer?" Amina stood and said to her teacher and her class,

> My father is a farmer. He has a big orchard of oranges, mangoes and guavas from where we get fruit juice. He also has a big poultry and animal farm where we get meat and eggs to eat, and he also has plenty of workers who are working on the farm. When I grow up, I want to be a farmer like my father, so that I can help plenty of families to get work and to also produce plenty of fruit juice, meat and eggs for my family and for people to buy and eat.

"Wonderful!" Teacher John exclaimed. "Clap for her" and the whole class clapped for Amina and she sat down feeling proud of herself. Although Amina is a girl, she has a dream of becoming someone who will use farming as a work to help herself and to also help others.

An issue you will face now is the talk about who you want to become in the future. A career is simply the kind of work you want to do through your lifetime. The earlier you find out what you want to do in life or what you want to be, the better it will be for you. This is because having your mind prepared allows you to identify, focus and maximize resources and opportunities.

Anyone who doesn't have a target will not know what to aim at. Many did not pay attention to this while they were young, only to grow old to fumble and gamble at what they would like to become. Unfortunately, those people hardly live to be happy doing what they do. Here are a few helpful tips towards choosing the right career for you.

Know Yourself

Find out the things you enjoy doing even without being asked. What's your favorite subject, the one that even if you fail, you still like? For example, do you like singing, writing, painting, teaching, plaiting or farming? What do you love to do? You could make that your career. You might like to know why you don't do other things you love to do so well. Who knows? You could make it easier someday for others.

Ask Questions

Isaac Newton was sitting under an apple tree reading his book one day. An apple fell to the ground near him and he picked it up and asked, "Why did this apple fall to the ground?" The answer he found to that question resulted in great discoveries in physics and mathematics. Men can travel to the moon and beyond today because, somebody had asked a good question and found an answer to it. Those who ask questions (we mean good questions) stand a good chance of becoming better learners and leaders.

Ask good questions of teachers, parents and guardians, and ask yourself too. Check online too because now there are many online resources to help students assess their interests and their skill sets to guide them toward good career fits. Ask questions about careers, questions like, "What must I know to become this or that?" "What kind of further schooling will I need for this career?" "If I should study this or that course, where will I work?" "What kind of work will I do?" "If I am doing this work, will I feel fulfilled?" Also, try to find relevance between what you want to do and how you can use it to help others. Find answers to questions such as; 'How can I use my career, job, or education to be of help to others around me?' Dare to try new things.

Be Prepared and Determined

When you have gotten satisfactory answers and information regarding what you truly desire to do in life, put in your whole effort. At times, your choice of career may change, but do not let the change be because of negative reasons. If you must change it, let it be because of something positive. Challenges and difficulties are certain on the way to anything worth doing because **nothing good comes easy.** You should also devote your time to the practice of those things you believe in. The quality of time you devote to your study, and practice of those things you like will determine the quality of the thing you will produce.

Therefore, as you put your effort to work toward your dreams, face it with all determination.

Put God in Your Plans

Whatever be your passion, ambition or goal, always do your best to see how to use it in service to God and helping others. If you can't do these, your labor will, at the end, be in vain. God gave us all we desire and all we will acquire (James 1:17). At the end, when He will test all things by the fire, only those things done for His glory will survive. Don't let your motivation be selfish and greedy for things like money, pleasure and fame. Many have lived for such and have concluded that it was vanity. They had wished they had lived for something better. God said we should lay up our treasures in heaven where we will find them (Matthew 6:19-21). He also said we should not work for the things that will perish, but for the ones that will last, which is his kingdom and righteousness.

If you desire to be an athlete, civil servant, soldier, tailor, politician, writer or whatever it may be, desire it, inquire about it, prepare for it, and be determined to work at it all for the glory of God (1Corinthians 10:31).

Discussion Points

1. Discuss which of these is a major motivation for career choice among young people; Money, Self-fulfillment, Fame, Ambition, Desire to help others and make things better, Selfishness and Ignorance.
2. What is supposed to be the most appropriate motivation as discussed in this chapter?
3. Do you have guidance counselors in your school? Should each secondary school have a team of qualified guidances counselors?
4. List and discuss some ways you think your career interest could help affect others positively.

CHAPTER 6

SELF ESTEEM

Doris and Esther are two different people. Doris thinks she is beautiful, intelligent and that she can be whatever she wants to become. Because of this, she has been having good scores in class. Esther, on the other hand, thinks she is not beautiful and is not intelligent. She thinks she is dull and cannot do anything good. This has made her not to have friends who like her and she has not been doing well in her class. The difference between the two girls is the issue of self-esteem or self-image, and this is what we want to talk to you about at this point.

One tool I am sure you will need to be a successful teenager is good self-esteem. First as a woman, I want you to be proud of who you are, where you come from, what you can do and even what you can't do. Do not let anyone look down on you. Never tell yourself you cannot do it. Do not accept anything as a hindrance.

Let me explain to you what self-esteem means. It is the expression of approval or disapproval of oneself and indicates the extent to which a person believes in himself or herself, her capabilities, skills, significance and ability to succeed.

A person with high self-esteem – not someone who is proud and pompous about himself or herself – has a fairly high opinion of herself and her abilities, and usually shows it in these ways:

- Such a person believes she can do it. She has confidence & competence.
- Such a person is responsible i.e. takes on assigned roles and tasks well.
- It makes one to earn the respect of others.
- It enables one to cope with challenges better.
- It also makes one think and feel good about oneself.

On the other hand, people with low self-esteem are the poorly motivated persons with the following characteristics:

- Critical
- Sometimes rebellious
- Unable to resist peer pressure
- Suspicious of people
- Wanting to please other people
- Believing they don't measure up to others or are inferior in some way
- Find difficulty in expressing their feelings
- Allows self to be pushed around
- Feels disliked and unwanted
- Feels helpless and inadequate
- Ineffective
- Often blame others
- Moody
- Withdrawn and isolated

You see, being a woman is nothing to be ashamed of. As matter of fact it is worth being proud of. If gender will be of any importance in the life to come, and if God will give the chance, many women would beg to be created as women again. I have understood that for a woman to become anything meaningful to herself, her family, community or society, she must also have the same attitude of appreciating and believing in who she was created to be: a woman. This is not pride, or looking down on others; rather it is saying

> God has given me all it takes to be who I am created to be, I am grateful and I am proud of it. I will use what I have to the uttermost.

That is high self-esteem.

I love to see women stand tall in those places where men think women cannot reach. This however, cannot happen unless the woman understands her value.

Women are special creations. Women bore and raised the kings. Womanhood is never a curse. It is not a mistake to be a woman. Womanhood is a blessing.

Dear, if you do not appreciate who you are it will be hard for you to work for progress. ***The journey into tomorrow begins today.*** You must appreciate your now before you can do so in the future. Never look down upon yourself. Never bring yourself so cheap and low because you are valuable and have a purpose in life. Do not let anyone intimidate you with intelligence, money or anything.

Being poor, weak or sick is never a disadvantage to anything. Helen Keller was blind from childhood, deaf and dumb, yet she lived, was happy, wrote books and was even a teacher. Fanny Crosby was a blind little girl who grew to write about eight thousand (8000) hymns. Were they held down by disabilities? No! It is not who you are or where you come from, your condition or circumstances that should define you. ***What makes the difference is what you believe about yourself.***

If it is true that a woman's education ends in the kitchen (like it's been said, especially in Africa), then I think kitchens such as the Presidential and Prime Minsters offices of countries like Liberia, Brazil, Argentina, Central African Republic, Switzerland, South Korea and

Germany to mention a few are good kitchens for the women (who had been and are still) in some of those places. Maybe the NAFDAC Director and Minister's offices are all good kitchens that late Prof. Mrs. Dora Akumyili had occupied, or consider Ngozi Oknojo Iwaela, I don't mind these types of kitchens myself.

Those whose education led them to a smoke-filled kitchen rather than the ones listed above or the international chef's kitchen must have been girls who had been made to believe they could not do it or did not have what it takes to make an impact in their time and they believed it. Did God make a mistake in creating them? Then why do they believe such lies and live by them? My dear, do not be misled by any of such lies.

Our African cultures tend to make women feel inferior to men. Women are treated as subservient to man. This results in discriminations such as: not being sent to school, being sent into marriage even if they don't like it, and a host of other improper treatments. It is true that the woman was created after the man was created, and that the man is to "rule" over the woman because the Bible says so (Genesis 3:16). However, this happened because of the sin our first parents Adam and Eve committed. God originally created man and woman as equals, both in His image, without any differentiation. None was less human before God. (Genesis 1:27) The differences are in terms of roles, duties and responsibilities. But does this call for treating women poorly as our cultural practices encourage? Think about this. Through Jesus, God has made all things right and has called all men to behave in the way he has intended. Bible passages like Ephesians 5:23-33 and 1 Peter 3:1-7, teach men to treat women with love and respect. Yet our cultural practices have allowed and encouraged men to continue to behave sinfully towards women. I pray things will change. It is good that you know this so that you can know the truth that will set you free. Do not, however, use this knowledge as a means of becoming rebellious and arrogant. Instead, let it humble you, and make you behave right. I pray that if it is in God's will for you to marry that you will find a man who will live out God's pattern of being a good husband, who will treat you with the dignity and respect all humans deserve.

I wish I could write you more on the specialty of being a woman. However, I want you to take note that it is not making it to the TV or becoming a national figure that shows you are a success. No! Rather, it is all about creating positive impact where you are. Like poor Tabitha did. She was a great help to the poor around her. What she did, although small, is still remembered until today (Acts 9:36-43). Never accept lies. Believe in who you are because you are special and God has created you for a special purpose in your time. Whenever the feelings of low self-esteem come your way, say these words to yourself (if possible, aloud),

> I am not what others say I am, I am not what I say I am, I am who God says I am. God says I am strong, he says I can, he says he is with me. Therefore, I will not be afraid.

Remember scriptures like 2 Timothy 1:7, "For God did not give us a spirit of timidity, but of power, of love and of self-discipline." And "I can do everything through Him (Christ) who gives me strength" (Philippians 4:13).

A website (Freedom in Christ Ministries) made a list of some truths we all need to know about ourselves. In this case we believe it will help you in building good self-image and to spot all the lies that may be thrown at you. Using the Bible they mentioned that if you are a Christian you are accepted...

With these truth revealed we say:

> *If God says 'You can', who can say you can't! Only you can stop yourself.*

Discussion Points

1. Who is your hero or heroine? What role did he/she play or is currently playing in affecting people positively?
2. Discuss some of the positive contributions women have made in the societies today, and how that has challenged or encouraged you.
3. Discuss the areas you may want to make a difference in and why.
4. List some women you know who began with little things and made significant differences.
5. What will you say of a woman who is not confident in who she is and in what she does? What advice will you give such a person?
6. Identify some of the beliefs you may have about yourself that do not line up to the valuable creature God made you to be (i.e. "I am worthless." "Other people are better than me." "I don't deserve to succeed.") Study Psalm 139 to learn what God says is true about His creation. It is helpful to identify lies about yourself you have believed. Root them out of your thinking patterns and replace them with truths that God says about you from His Word!

CHAPTER 7

WHAT MATTERS MOST

Grandpa Obed was diagnosed with a terminal illness and was receiving care at the hospital. He was always in the company of his children, grandchildren and great grandchildren. Despite his sickness, Grandpa looked happy and also joked from time to time. A nurse attending to him once came to check on him and asked all the children out. Then she said to the sick old man, "You are a lucky and happy old man to have all these children with you at this time." In his usual funny nature, the old man replied, "Yes, I think I am indeed." Then he continued, "You know despite all that God has given me in this life," then he coughed and continued again, "there is one thing for which I am eternally grateful, which is worth much more than all put together." This made the nurse curious. After she had helped him swallow his medicine she said, "That must have been your wife." The old man beamed with smile and said, "Yes I am grateful for time I shared with my late wife," and the nurse apologized, "I'm sorry I didn't know your wife was dead." He answered, "Don't worry that was eight years ago." The nurse then said, "You must rest now" and began walking out. But the old man said "I thought you might be interested to know what that thing is?" She returned.

It is the joy of knowing that in all my years of toils and labour,
God has given the one thing that matters most. That is the gift
of eternal life.

Then he smiled again and looked at the nurse and said, "That is why I am sure I will see my Katrina again."

As you face these teen years, many things will present themselves as very important, needing your attention. Matters such as succeeding in your studies, keeping yourself away from being infected by teenage fevers, setting yourself as an example for others, and doing your best to protect yourself for the future. All these are of great importance, but we both want to talk to you about an issue that matters most in life, not only to you as a teenager, but to everyone alive as well.

God is the Creator of everything we see. Take a look at His mighty works. For instance, He protects us in our mother's wombs, from diseases when we were still babies and many things we cannot count in our lives today. Look at the sky, the birds, trees and all of His creation. He made them all for us so that we can enjoy them.

He did all this because He loves us and He still wants to show us more of his love.

In the beginning, God created Adam and Eve in the Garden of Eden, and their relationship was good and lovely. However, this sweet relationship was broken because the Devil deceived them into disobeying God by breaking His commandments. As a result, sin came into the world and blocked our relationship with God. The Bible says in Romans 3:23, "For all have sinned and fall short of the glory of God" (NIV) And God declares the punishment of sin to be death (Romans 6:23).

Because God loves us so much, He sent His son to die for us to take away the punishment of our sins, so that we can get back to God and enjoy the good life He has for us. His plan for you is to have the best of your teen years, to grow and experience the good things He desires for you. He also wants you to be with Him in heaven when you die one day. Satan on the other hand wants to destroy what God has for you as he did with Adam and Eve. That is why he introduces the teenage fevers and other bad things so as to keep you from reaching them.

However, the only way you can get to God and fully enjoy the good life He has for you is to believe in the One He sent to save the whole world; Jesus Christ. Whoever believes in Christ will not face the second death of hell fire, but will have eternal life. Many have rejected him and have believed in other people; others believe in objects like the sun, moon and stars. The sad story about such people is that they only die and go to hell. ***Jesus alone is the only way to eternal life.*** Many have misunderstood how to accept and believe in Him; they think because they bear Christian names, go to church, crusades, concerts, camps, give offerings and tithes and participate in other Christian activities, that that makes them Christians. It is not true. The only way we can escape death and become Christians, is by personally accepting Jesus as our Savior. We must each say it with our mouth and believe what we say in our hearts; that is what actually makes us Christians.

This is why it is important to say and believe a prayer like this:

> *Lord Jesus, I admit that I am a sinner, and I cannot save myself unless I believe and accept you as my personal Saviour and Lord. Please come into my heart now, forgive my sins and make me your child. Thank you for answering my prayer. Amen.*

Whatever wrong we have committed, Jesus is willing to come and forgive them. Whoever has not believed this in his heart and confessed it with his mouth is yet to be saved. The Bible says,

> That if you confess with your mouth, "Jesus is Lord," and believe in your heart that God raised Him from the dead, you will be saved. For it is with your heart that you believe and are

justified, and it is with your mouth that you confess and are saved.

—Romans 10:9-10

This life we live will one day come to an end, but the big question is: Where will you spend your eternity? Have you asked yourself this important question?

If you have said and believed the prayer above, congratulations. You can rest assured that you are God's child. If you have not, what are you waiting for? This is a good opportunity for you to do so. Jesus is waiting. He said,

> Here I am! I stand at the door [of your heart] and knock. If anyone hears my voice and opens the door, I will come in and eat with him, and he with me.

—Revelation 3:20

Whatever you will become and whatever you will do in life, this is the most important issue of life. You can always depend on Jesus to be able to live a good and respectable life, because that is what he came to give.

If you have made the decision of making Jesus your Saviour and Lord, you will need to know the ways to maintain a close relationship with him. We cannot just claim to be God's children (Christians) and yet not have a good relationship with our father. One sure way to do this is to;

Communicate with God daily

To keep a relationship strong among friends, family members, and in a group is ensuring effective communication. This is also true of the relationship with God. You will need to always communicate with God. Some of the ways to communicate with God include the following:

- *Prayer:* Prayer can simply mean talking with God. The Bible says we should pray always (1 Thessalonians 5:17). The *always* means without restriction to place or time. Now this means you can talk with God anytime and in any place. And when you talk with God, who is your Father, feel free to tell Him about everything in your life. Let Him know when you are happy, sad, afraid or confused. Furthermore, when you are talking with God, always praise Him by reminding yourself of the good things about His character or things He has done. Also, do not continue praying without letting Him know the wrongs you have done. Do not forget to thank Him _in_ (not for) all the things you are going through, whether you like them or not. This is because we are to give thanks to Him _in_ all situations (1 Thessalonians 5:18). And always tell Him your problems, no matter how big or little they may be. However, as you talk to Him, learn to pay attention. Listen carefully; He could also be gently talking back to you. We will tell you more about listening in a little while.

  Praying can also be accompanied by fasting. Fasting is simply setting aside time to abstain from food and drink in order to hear God more clearly regarding things you want Him to act upon. There is no time limit to fasting; it could be abstaining from breakfast only, breakfast and lunch or for a whole day. It could also mean refusing some pleasurable activities such as watching television, but the point, is that fasting will not make much meaning without prayer and reading the Bible.

- *Through the Bible:* The only way to get to know the will of God and to hear Him is to read His word. Spend time reading the Bible, memorize portions of it and meditate on it, i.e., spend some time to think deeply about the meaning of the things you have read. By so doing, you will hear God give you directions on things to do and on how to do them.

- *Through your devotions:* This is setting apart a time in a quiet place to specially commune and relate with God just like Jesus did in Mark 1:35. For a quiet time, you will need a Bible, a devotional guide and a book or a jotter to write down special things you think God is personally telling you to note.

    One key thing you should notice is that throughout the entire process of communicating with God, listening is very important. As you listen more to God, you'll become familiar with his voice, you'll get closer to him and your life will become shaped into his plan for you. Listening is very important because it can affect our lives greatly, positively or negatively. It depends on what you are listening to. Give careful attention to the things you listen to because there are many bad and wrong things that will come your way. Satan, our enemy, sends these things so that we cannot hear God clearly or at all. Now, those who spend their time listening to secular music will become worldly in their thoughts and actions, but those who listen to God will become godly. Therefore, be careful what you listen to, because it will shape your life.

- *Fellowship:* All of the ways listed above are means to fellowshipping with God. However, God intends that for us to grow, we need the fellowship of one another as well. To fellowship means the condition of being together or of sharing similar interests or experiences. You can find this fellowship in church, and by engaging in activities of Christian groups. Fellowship is very important because you will find help, comfort, support, encouragement, correction, and rebuke from those around you. It will also be an opportunity for you to discover and use your spiritual gifts to help others grow. Proverbs 27:17 says, "As iron sharpens iron, so one man sharpens another." We need God and one another to grow in our Christian faith.

BYE

We may not have written all that is required because we are humans and have shortcomings.

We hope you have been encouraged by our long letter and it has motivated you to positively use your wonderful teenage years and sail forward in your youth to achieve success.

We love you and we hope to write to you more.

Affectionately yours,
Dominic and Achsah Asedeh.

BIBLIOGRAPHY

If you desire to find and read some of the resources we consulted to help us in writing to you, here they are.

Dillon, Carotta, Michael Valerie Vance. *Growing Up Sexually.* Winona, Minnesota: Saint Mary's Press, 1989.

Ginout, Haim G. *Between Parent and Teenagers.* Ontario: The Macmillan Company, 1969.

Lewis, Gregg and Deborah Shaw. *Today's Heroes.* Jos, Nigeria: Tishbeth Publishers, 2002.

Meroff, Deborah. *True Grit.* London: Authentic Media, 2006.

Newman, Barbara M., Philip R. Newman. *Development Through Life.* Pacific Groove, California: Brooks/Cole pub. Company, 1991.

Poonen, Annie Zac. *A Girl's Viewpoint.* Jos, Nigeria: Tishbeth Publishers, 1999.

Taylor, Kenneth N. *Growing Up.* Bukuru, Jos: ACTS, 1995.

Walsh, Mike (Editor). *Clinical Nursing and Related Sciences.* Edinburg: Bailliere Tindal, 2002.

Walt, Mueller. *Understanding Today's Youth.* Wheaton, Il: Tyndale House, 1994.

Waugh, Anne and Allison Grant. *Anatomy and Physiology in Health and Illness.* Edinburg, Churchill: Livingstone, 2001.

Life Skill Manual (a Life Skill Manual for Youth in Secondary Schools and Churches). Nigeria: A work of SUWA and FCS, 2006.

http://images.tutorvista.com/content/reproduction/female-reproductive-system.jpeg .

ficm.org (Freedominchristministries.com).

www.ingramcontent.com/pod-product-compliance
Lightning Source LLC
Chambersburg PA
CBHW071228130726
47998CB00002B/877